TODDLER
meal
PLANNER

Nicola Graimes

p

This is a Parragon Publishing Book

First published in 2001

Parragon Publishing
Queen Street House
4 Queen Street
Bath, BA1 1HE UK

Copyright © Parragon 2001

Designed by THE BRIDGEWATER BOOK COMPANY

Art Director Terry Jeavons
Editorial Director Fiona Biggs
Senior Designer Colin Fielder
Editor Sarah Bragginton
Page Design Jane Lanaway
Picture Research Liz Moore
Photography David Jordan
Home Economist Sarah Lewis
Illustrations Rhian Nest-James

Printed and bound in Spain

ISBN 0-75255-208-2

This book uses metric and imperial measurements. Follow
the same units of measurement throughout; do not mix metric
and imperial. All spoon measurements are level: teaspoons are
assumed to be 5 ml and tablespoons are assumed to be 15 ml.
Unless otherwise stated, milk is assumed to be full fat, eggs and
individual vegetables such as potatoes are medium, and pepper
is freshly ground black pepper.

The times given for each recipe are an approximate guide
only because the preparation times may differ according to the
techniques used by different people and the cooking times may
vary as a result of the type of oven used.

contents

SECTION ONE
eighteen to thirty-six months

SECTION TWO
three to four years

SECTION THREE
four plus

Introduction

It is perfectly common for a toddler's food preferences to change—even on a daily basis. Infants who previously ate just about anything you offered may start to develop apparently peculiar likes and dislikes. This is the age group where mealtimes can become a challenge—though with the right approach, you can minimize any hiccups!

If your toddler happily eats everything that is presented before him or her, then you are an incredibly lucky parent. Most of us are much less fortunate. Nevertheless, so long as you are prepared for the ups and downs, this can be a fun and rewarding time. At this stage, weaning should be firmly established— your toddler can now eat the same foods as you, usually making it unnecessary to prepare separate meals. Additionally, sterilizing eating utensils and puréeing foods are now in the distant past (although good hygiene practices are still absolutely crucial).

Most importantly, don't worry if your toddler refuses to try some foods. However stressful mealtimes can be, it is vital to keep calm and be patient. Toddlers have an uncanny ability to pick up on their parents' anxieties and mealtimes can become battles of will. Most toddlers can be very fickle; their likes and dislikes can change, even on a daily basis, which can be extremely frustrating if you've spent time and energy lovingly preparing homecooked food, but it's crucial not to try and force your child to eat as this can affect attitudes to food later in life.

Toddlers have a strong desire for independence and mealtimes can be a perfect time to exercise it. At this stage, it is important to nurture and encourage this

ABOVE *It's fun for your child to help you with meals and learn about how food makes its way to the table.*

LEFT *Your toddler will now want to use his or her own cutlery—encourage this growing self-confidence in your child.*

growing sense of self. Allow your child to feed him or herself or at least offer a second spoon—it's all part of the fun! By doing so, you are preparing your toddler for times ahead: for example, starting nursery or school.

The aim of this book is to ease any anxieties you may have about meals and mealtimes, and smooth the transition from toddler to young child. The recipes have been designed to appeal to young children and adults alike, with the odd concession to nutritious versions of so-called "children's food." I've tried to include a wide range of dishes, incorporating a variety of cuisines, flavors, and textures. The meal plans will help you to balance your child's diet on a daily and weekly basis. Treat these as guidelines—you don't have to stick to them rigidly.

It's easy to become bogged down in the intricacies of providing a balanced diet, but good, nutritious food does not have to be complicated to prepare or take long to cook. Nothing could be easier than a baked potato with a dollop of pesto or houmus. Canned beans, such as garbanzo beans or kidney beans, and frozen vegetables, including spinach and peas, add substance and nutritional value to soups, stews, risottos, and pasta dishes. Conjure up different ways of serving vegetables. Often raw vegetables are more popular than cooked, and they're healthier. Additionally, if time allows, encourage your toddler to join in the cooking—I've found they're more likely to try the results. Food should be fun; after all, eating is one of the great pleasures in life!

What Does My Toddler Need?

Children over a year old can join in family meals, but their requirement for high-energy foods is still much greater than that of adults. Compared with the very rapid growth rate during the first year, your toddler is now growing more slowly. However, you'll find that he or she is far more active—walking, jumping, and running—which means that extra calories and a varied, nutritious diet are essential for growth and development.

The term "balanced diet" can intimidate even the most nutritionally aware parent. Yet as long as your toddler is eating a good mix of foods, including bread, pasta, rice, potatoes, fruits and vegetables, dairy foods, meat, fish, and eggs, preferably on a daily or, if not, on a weekly basis, then that should be more than sufficient. Obviously this range of foods can vary depending on special diets, eating preferences, and the presence of any food intolerances or allergies. Choose foods from the food groups detailed below and your toddler will almost certainly get all the nutrients he or she needs:

STARCHY FOODS

Starchy foods, otherwise known as carbohydrates, include breakfast cereals, bread, pasta, rice, and potatoes. These should form a major part of your

LEFT *Offer raw vegetables and fruit as a snack instead of cookies or cake.*

toddler's diet as they are a good source of energy, fiber, vitamins, and minerals. Whole-grain varieties, such as whole-wheat bread, brown rice, and pasta, provide the richest source of nutrients and fiber, yet should not be given in large amounts to young children. Unlike adults, toddlers find it difficult to digest large amounts of high-fiber foods, leading to stomach upsets and a reduced appetite. Fiber can also interfere with the absorption of certain minerals.

FRUITS AND VEGETABLES

Fresh and frozen fruits and vegetables, more so than canned, are an essential part of a toddler's diet, providing rich amounts of vitamins, minerals, and fiber. Try to offer around four to five

ABOVE *Your child will become increasingly active and have high energy levels.*

different types of fresh produce a day, such as citrus fruit, salad, and orange, red, and green vegetables, to ensure a good balance of nutrients.

Many children refuse to eat cooked vegetables—mainly because of their different texture—but will happily try raw sticks of carrot, red bell pepper, and celery or lightly steamed snow peas, baby corn, and broccoli, especially if dipped in houmus, guacamole, garlic butter, or mayonnaise. Presenting vegetables in various guises also seems to work. Try them puréed in soups and sauces, combined with mashed potatoes, or grated into patties or burgers.

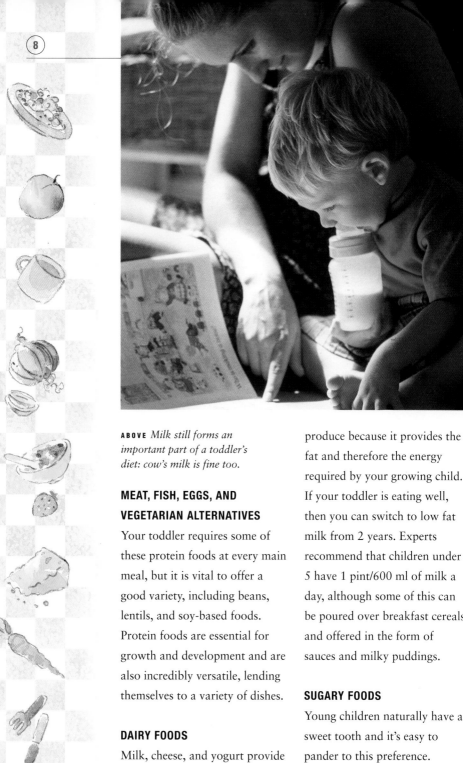

ABOVE *Milk still forms an important part of a toddler's diet: cow's milk is fine too.*

MEAT, FISH, EGGS, AND VEGETARIAN ALTERNATIVES

Your toddler requires some of these protein foods at every main meal, but it is vital to offer a good variety, including beans, lentils, and soy-based foods. Protein foods are essential for growth and development and are also incredibly versatile, lending themselves to a variety of dishes.

DAIRY FOODS

Milk, cheese, and yogurt provide protein, vitamins, and minerals, particularly calcium for healthy bones and teeth. Although cow's milk can be used in cooking from 6 months, it's suitable as a drink from 1 year. Opt for whole dairy

produce because it provides the fat and therefore the energy required by your growing child. If your toddler is eating well, then you can switch to low fat milk from 2 years. Experts recommend that children under 5 have 1 pint/600 ml of milk a day, although some of this can be poured over breakfast cereals and offered in the form of sauces and milky puddings.

SUGARY FOODS

Young children naturally have a sweet tooth and it's easy to pander to this preference. Unfortunately, sugary foods, including chocolate, candy, cakes, cookies, and fizzy drinks, rot the teeth and spoil a child's appetite for healthier alternatives. It can be a challenge to curb a child's desire for sweet foods, especially when presented with aisles of sugary delights while grocery shopping, but try to start as you mean to go on. Look for healthier alternatives to the above, but don't resort to those containing artificial sweeteners, since they've been found to cause upset stomachs if eaten in excess. Nevertheless, an outright ban on sweet foods can backfire, making them even more desirable to your toddler: the answer seems to be to offer sugary things in moderation.

IRON

Iron deficiency is common, especially among women and children. The mineral is essential for the healthy development of mind and body and a deficiency can lead to tiredness, irritability, anemia, and a poor immune system. Iron absorption can be enhanced by accompanying a meal with a glass of fresh orange juice. Red meat and liver, fish, eggs, beans and lentils, some fruits and vegetables, whole-grain cereals, fortified breakfast cereals, and dried fruit are all good sources of iron.

FATTY FOODS

Children need a higher proportion of fat in their diets than adults, both for energy and development. This does not mean that children thrive on high-fat pastries, cookies, cakes, potato chips, and fried foods, but do try, at least up to the age of 5, to offer whole dairy products, oils of vegetable origin, lean meat, skinless chicken, and oily fish such as salmon, tuna, mackerel, sardines, and herrings. Avoid hydrogenated fats, found in many processed foods, including pies, sausages, and cookies, since they are just as bad for us as saturated fats. Grilling, poaching, and baking foods are preferable.

SALTY FOODS

Cut down on salt as much as possible, especially as this seasoning is found naturally in many foods and is also added to many commercial products. If cooking for the whole family, remove your child's portion before adding any salt.

LEFT *Toddlers naturally have a sweet tooth, but try to offer sugary foods in moderation.*

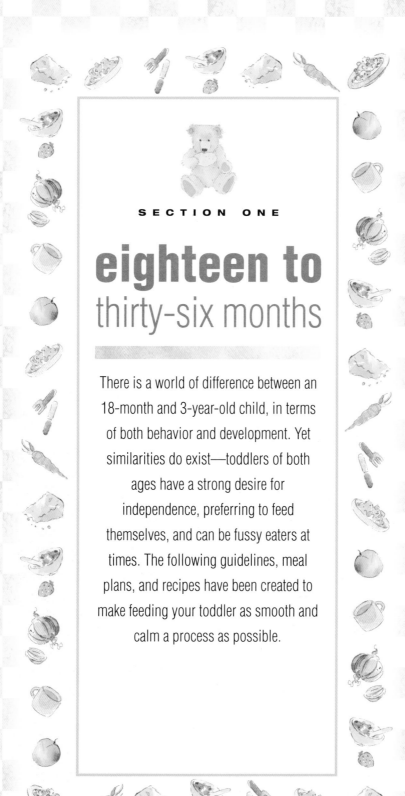

SECTION ONE

eighteen to
thirty-six months

There is a world of difference between an
18-month and 3-year-old child, in terms
of both behavior and development. Yet
similarities do exist—toddlers of both
ages have a strong desire for
independence, preferring to feed
themselves, and can be fussy eaters at
times. The following guidelines, meal
plans, and recipes have been created to
make feeding your toddler as smooth and
calm a process as possible.

Good Eating Habits

Many nutritionists believe that good eating habits are formed in early childhood, so it is essential to encourage your toddler to try (and hopefully enjoy) a variety of foods, encompassing a range of flavors, colors, and textures, when he or she is as young as possible. However, it's never too late to make healthy changes to your toddler's diet.

FRESH IS BEST

In an ideal world, only homecooked foods would pass our little ones' lips, yet this is unrealistic for most us. The biggest influence on our children's health is the quality and variety of ingredients used and, perhaps reassuringly, not all prepared foods are bad. The foods you should avoid are those where saturated or hydrogenated fats, colorings, additives, sweeteners, sugar, and salt appear high in the ingredients list. Try to get into the habit of reading the list of ingredients and the nutritional information on the package before you buy it.

Having said this, a toddler's diet shouldn't rely on processed foods, and it is crucial to introduce freshly prepared meals at as young an age as possible. Habits are formed early and it's easier to avoid junk foods while children are small. Toddlers will inevitably turn their noses up at some foods, but the more choice they are given, the better—both for them and you.

Researchers at the University of Birmingham, England, have found that young children are more open to new tastes and flavors than is sometimes assumed. Additionally, fresh foods don't have to take long to prepare, usually taste better than junk foods, and are more nutritious. If this wasn't enough to convince you, they're usually cheaper: with convenience foods you are actually paying someone else to do the work!

EATING TOGETHER

There are numerous reasons why it is not always possible for the family to eat together. However, you'll reap the benefits in the long term, even if you manage communal mealtimes only at the weekend. For the rest of the week, try at least to sit down with your toddler while he or she is eating, and perhaps have your own small portion of food. Toddlers learn by example and it also makes mealtimes a more enjoyable and social affair. Incidentally, try to ignore poor eating habits and you'll probably find your toddler will soon get bored with playing up. Instead, offer heaps of praise and encouragement when your toddler eats well.

SNACK TIME

While some toddlers refuse to eat a complete meal, most relish snacks, especially if they can feed themselves. Take advantage of this by offering healthy snacks. This may be a way of supplementing an otherwise restricted diet. The following ideas may help when you are faced with a hungry toddler:

ABOVE *If you eat plenty of fresh fruit, your children should follow by example and accept this as normal.*

- Wedges of raw fruit and vegetables
- Rice cakes with low-salt yeast extract
- Slices of pita bread with smooth peanut butter
- Fruit muffins with banana
- Plain yogurt with honey
- Breadsticks with houmus
- Soft tortilla with guacamole
- Flapjacks
- Fruit scones
- Homemade popcorn
- Fingers of pineapple with cream cheese
- Homemade vegetable crisps
- Dried fruit and nuts
- Carrot cake
- Low-salt tortilla chips, covered with grated cheese and broiled
- Oatcakes and pâté.

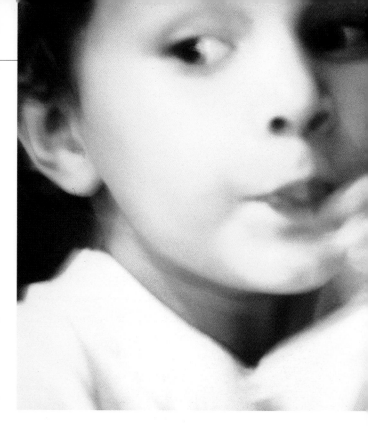

Establishing a Routine

All toddlers are different—some take to eating three main meals a day, others prefer to snack. Both are acceptable at this stage, although, as your toddler becomes older, it is advisable to introduce a pattern of regular eating times. Try to make mealtimes fun and not a time of conflict and tension.

THREE MEALS A DAY

Work on establishing a regular eating pattern, based on three main meals, plus a couple of snacks a day. Even this can take time and patience to establish, however, so don't despair. If "grazing" is preferred by your toddler, make sure that he or she is offered a varied selection of healthy snacks (see page 13) based on high-energy, nutritious foods.

Toddlers have small stomachs and require regular, small meals to keep them going. Don't worry if he or she sometimes doesn't seem hungry, or even skips a meal: as long as your toddler is gaining weight and also growing and developing well, then there should be no need for concern.

A healthy diet should be based on fruits and vegetables, bread, pasta, rice, potatoes, breakfast

LEFT Replace some of your child's milk intake with homemade fruit smoothies or unsweetened fruit juice.

meal. This doesn't mean that you have to spend hours painstakingly arranging every meal on the plate, but try to make meals look as inviting as possible. Bright colors, different textures, and a range of shapes make all the difference, as do interesting plates, eating utensils, bibs, and mats.

DRINKS

Milk should still form an important part of your child's diet, since it provides a valuable combination of energy, protein, calcium, iron, zinc, and vitamins. Cola, fizzy drinks, tea, coffee, and sweetened fruit juices and squash should be avoided if possible. Sugar-laden drinks rot the teeth, curb the appetite, and lead to weight gain. However, low-sugar alternatives that contain artificial sweeteners are often no better, and can upset the stomach if drunk in excess. Water, diluted unsweetened fruit juices, and homemade versions are the preferred option.

Smoothies, made from puréed fruit, milk, and/or yogurt, freshly squeezed juices, and homemade hot chocolate (cubes of good-quality chocolate melted into hot milk) all make nutritious, comforting drinks.

cereals, meat, fish, eggs, and whole dairy produce, with the occasional sweet treat. You may obviously have to make allowances for personal preferences and special diets.

There is now no need to purée or mash foods—your toddler should be getting used to, or be familiar with, chewing and with the sometimes unfamiliar texture of solid foods. Some young children dislike lumps, whether meat, fruit, or vegetables, and grinding or finely chopping such foods may make them much more acceptable.

PRESENTATION

Imaginative and attractive presentation can make the difference between a toddler eating or refusing even to try a

MEAL PLANNER 1

18-36 MONTHS	BREAKFAST	LUNCH
Day 1	Ready Brek, toast, milk	Creamy smoked salmon & broccoli pasta Baked peach crumbles
Day 2	Hard-cooked egg, toast, melon, milk	Spicy rice balls with tomato Vegetables Banana custard scrunch
Day 3	Weetabix and banana Fruit bread, milk	Starfish pie, peas Baked apple & custard
Day 4	Porridge & grated apple Toast, milk	Pork & apple casserole Potatoes & vegetables Plain yogurt
Day 5	Pancakes with fruit filling Yogurt, milk	Potato & cabbage patties Peas and broiled sausage Ice cream
Day 6	Cereal & raisins, toast, milk	Pasta and vegetables in cheese sauce Baked peach crumbles
Day 7	Diced bacon & broiled tomatoes on toast Yogurt, milk	Roast joint (or vegetarian alternative), roast potatoes and vegetables Rice pudding with raisins

TEA	SUPPER
Pizza fingers Houmus & vegetable sticks Yogurt	Sardines on toast Fruit Milky drink
Crispy chicken fingers & coleslaw Strawberry & vanilla yogurt ice	Cheese on toast Fruit Milky drink
Hearty bean & pasta soup Garlic bread Mini banana & chocolate muffins	Sandwich Fruit Milky drink
Baked potato with tuna & sweetcorn Strawberry ice lolly	Scrambled egg with muffin Fruit & milky drink
Eggy bread and beans Flapjack	Guacamole with tortilla/pita bread Vegetable sticks Fruit & milky drink
Spicy rice balls/chicken sticks with houmus and tortilla Crunchy nut coleslaw Strawberry & vanilla yogurt ice	Sandwich Fruit Milky drink
Tuna and cheese on toast Vegetable sticks Banana custard scrunch	Apple muffins Fruit Milky drink

Hearty Bean & Pasta Soup

PREPARATION TIME *10 minutes* **COOKING TIME** *40 minutes*
FREEZING *suitable, but omit Parmesan cheese* **SERVES** *4 adults*

This wholesome bean and pasta soup is substantial enough to be served as a meal in itself, providing a good, healthy balance of vegetables and pasta. Accompany it with buttery garlic bread.

❶ Heat the olive oil in a large, heavy-bottomed saucepan. Add the onion, celery, and carrot and cook over a medium heat for 8–10 minutes, stirring occasionally, until the vegetables have softened.

❷ Add the bay leaf, bouillon, and chopped tomatoes, then bring to a boil. Reduce the heat, cover and simmer for 15 minutes, or until the vegetables are tender.

❸ Add the pasta and beans, then bring the soup back to a boil and simmer for 10 minutes, or until the pasta is just tender. Stir occasionally to prevent the pasta sticking to the bottom of the pan and burning.

INGREDIENTS
4 tbsp olive oil
1 onion, finely chopped
1 celery stick, chopped
1 carrot, peeled and diced
1 bay leaf
5 cups vegetable bouillon
14 oz/400 g can chopped tomatoes
generous 1 cup pasta shapes, such as farfalle, shells or twists
14 oz/400 g can cannellini beans, drained and rinsed
salt and freshly ground black pepper
7 oz/200 g spinach or Swiss chard, thick stalks removed and shredded
1½ oz /40 g Parmesan cheese, finely grated

❹ Season to taste, add the spinach and cook for a further 2 minutes, or until tender. Serve, sprinkled with Parmesan cheese.

Creamy Smoked Salmon & Broccoli Pasta

PREPARATION TIME *10 minutes* **COOKING TIME** *15 minutes*

FREEZING *unsuitable* **SERVES** *4 adults*

Smoked salmon pieces are now readily available from food stores and fish suppliers and don't cost the earth. It is ideal for this dish as it has a slightly milder flavor and loses its oily texture when cooked, which seems to appeal to children.

❶ Cook the pasta according to the instructions on the package, until the pasta is tender, then drain. Meanwhile, steam the broccoli for 8–10 minutes, or until tender.

❷ At the same time, prepare the sauce. Heat the oil and butter in a small heavy-bottomed skillet, then add the leek and sauté for 7 minutes, or until softened. Gently stir in the cream cheese and milk and heat through.

INGREDIENTS

3½ cups pasta shells, bows, or tagliatelle

8 oz/225 g broccoli florets

1 tbsp olive oil

2 tbsp butter

1 leek, finely chopped

200 g tub garlic and herb cream cheese

6 tbsp whole milk

3½ oz/100 g smoked salmon pieces

salt and freshly ground black pepper

❸ Add the smoked salmon pieces and cook for a minute or so, until they turn opaque. Combine the sauce with the pasta and broccoli and mix together well. Season.

Pizza Fingers

PREPARATION TIME *15 minutes* **COOKING TIME** *25 minutes*

FREEZING *suitable* **SERVES** *2 adults*

This pizza is sliced into handy-sized pieces, which are perfect for little fingers to hold. I've given a choice of four toppings to give the pizza a chequerboard effect, but you can opt for one topping if preferred. Additionally, a ready-made foccacia or ciabatta is a good alternative to a homemade base.

❶ To make the pizza base, place the flour, salt, and yeast in a bowl. Make a well in the center of the flour and add the water and oil, then mix with a knife until the mixture forms a soft dough.

❷ Turn out on to a lightly floured counter and knead for 5 minutes. Cover and leave for 5 minutes. Knead again for 5 minutes until the dough is smooth and elastic. Place in a lightly oiled bowl and cover with plastic wrap. Leave in a warm place for 45 minutes, or until doubled in size.

❸ Preheat the oven to 425°F/220°C. To make the tomato sauce, heat the oil in a heavy-bottomed skillet and cook the garlic for 1 minute, or until softened. Add the strained tomatoes and sugar, then cook for 5–7 minutes, or until reduced and thickened. Stir in the oregano and seasoning, then set aside.

INGREDIENTS

2 tsp olive oil, plus extra for greasing and sprinkling

1 clove garlic, crushed

5 oz/140 g strained tomatoes

½ tsp sugar

½ tsp oregano

salt and freshly ground black pepper

1 cup mozzarella cheese

½ cup Cheddar cheese, grated

PIZZA BASE

2 cups white bread flour, sifted

1 tsp salt

½ tsp easy-blend yeast

⅔ cup warm water

1 tbsp olive oil

TOPPINGS

handful of cooked fresh spinach leaves, tough stalks removed, shredded, and squeezed dry

2¾ oz/75 g canned tuna in oil, drained

½ yellow or orange bell pepper, seeded and finely sliced

4 slices salami

4 Knead the risen dough lightly, then roll out to form a rough rectangle or place in an oiled rectangular-shaped pan. If you are not using a pan, place the base on a lightly oiled cookie sheet and push up the edges of the dough to form a shallow rim.

5 Spoon the tomato mixture over the base. Top one quarter of the base with the cooked spinach, a second quarter with tuna, a third quarter with the yellow bell pepper, and the remaining quarter with salami. Crumble the mozzarella cheese with your fingers and sprinkle it over the toppings. Repeat with the Cheddar cheese. Season and drizzle with a little olive oil.

6 Bake in the top of the oven for 12–15 minutes, until the topping is slightly crisp and golden. Slice into fingers before serving.

Pork & Apple Casserole

PREPARATION TIME *10 minutes* **COOKING TIME** *1 hour, 18 minutes*
FREEZING *suitable* **SERVES** *4 adults*

The apple adds a delicious sweetness and texture to this warming casserole, packed with tender pork pieces. It is a big hit served with a dollop of mashed potato or plain rice.

❶ 1 Preheat the oven to 350°F/180°C.

❷ Heat the oil in a heavy-bottomed skillet. Add the pork and cook for 5 minutes. Transfer to a casserole dish.

❸ Add the leeks to the pan and sauté for 5 minutes, or until softened, then add the carrots. Cook for a further 3 minutes, covered. Add the flour and cook for 1 minute, stirring well.

❹ Gradually add the bouillon, apple juice, mustard, bay leaf, and rosemary. Bring to the boil and cook for 2 minutes, stirring until thickened. Season to taste.

❺ Arrange the apple slices on top of the pork and pour the sauce over the top. Cover and cook for 1 hour, or until the pork is tender.

INGREDIENTS
1 tbsp olive oil
4 boneless pork loins, each weighing about 4 oz/115 g
2 leeks, finely sliced
2 carrots, peeled and finely chopped
1 tbsp all-purpose flour
scant 1 cup vegetable bouillon
¼ cup apple juice
2 tsp Dijon mustard
1 bay leaf
1 tbsp fresh rosemary, finely chopped
2 eating apples, peeled, cored, and sliced
salt and freshly ground black pepper

Crispy Chicken Fingers with Garlic Dip

PREPARATION TIME *15 minutes* **COOKING TIME** *8 minutes*

FREEZING *suitable* **MAKES** *6 fingers*

These polenta-encrusted chicken pieces are perfect finger food for toddlers, and they seem to enjoy dipping them into the garlic dip! Serve the goujons with Crunchy Nut Coleslaw (see page 26).

INGREDIENTS

¾ oz/20 g fine cornmeal or polenta

½ tsp paprika

salt and freshly ground black pepper

6 oz/175 g skinless chicken breast, cut into strips

1 tbsp olive oil

1 egg, beaten

vegetable oil, for sautéing

GARLIC DIP

6 tbsp mayonnaise

1 small clove garlic, crushed

good squeeze of fresh lemon juice

❶ First make the garlic dip. Put the mayonnaise, garlic, and lemon juice into a bowl and mix well.

❷ Put the cornmeal, paprika, and seasoning in a shallow bowl. Dip each piece of chicken into the olive oil, then the egg. Roll the chicken in the cornmeal mixture and shake to remove any crumbs.

❸ Heat enough oil to generously cover a heavy-bottomed skillet. Arrange the chicken pieces in the pan and cook for 2–3 minutes on each side until cooked and golden.

Starfish Pie

PREPARATION TIME *10 minutes*

COOKING TIME *45 minutes*

FREEZING *suitable*

SERVES *4 adults*

Golden puff-pie-dough shapes add a fun element to this fish pie, but you can opt for mashed potato if preferred. It's wise to sift through the pie with a fork before serving to ensure there are no stray bones.

INGREDIENTS
2 hard-cooked eggs
1 tbsp olive oil
1 onion, finely chopped
1 celery stick, finely chopped
1 carrot, peeled and finely chopped
small handful of spinach leaves, tough stalks removed and finely shredded
1 cup whole milk
4 tbsp heavy cream
½ cup sharp Cheddar cheese, grated
1 tsp Dijon mustard
2 tbsp finely chopped fresh parsley
squeeze of fresh lemon juice
salt and freshly ground black pepper
8 oz/225 g undyed smoked haddock, skin and bones removed, cut into pieces
8 oz/225 g cod fillet, skin and bones removed
1 sheet of ready-rolled puff pie dough, defrosted if using frozen
1 egg, beaten, to glaze

❶ Preheat the oven to 400°F/200°C.

❷ Heat the oil in a heavy-bottomed skillet. Add the onion and sauté for 5 minutes, or until softened, then add the celery and carrot and sauté for 3 minutes. Add the spinach and cook for a further 2 minutes, or until tender.

❸ Stir in the milk and cream and bring to a boil. Turn off the heat and stir in the Cheddar cheese, mustard, parsley, and lemon juice. Season to taste.

❹ Place the fish in an ovenproof dish. Peel and chop the egg and spoon it over the fish, then top with the creamy vegetable sauce.

❺ Place the pie dough on a lightly floured counter. Make fish and starfish shapes using cookie cutters, then arrange them on top of the creamy fish sauce. Brush the pie dough shapes with beaten egg and bake for 20–25 minutes, or until the fish is cooked and the pie dough shapes have risen and are a golden brown color.

Crunchy Nut Coleslaw

PREPARATION TIME *10 minutes*   **COOKING TIME** *1 minute*

FREEZING *unsuitable*   **SERVES** *2 adults*

The natural sweetness of the fruit in this pretty pink salad makes it appealing to toddlers. The scallion is optional and can be added if your child likes it. The coleslaw also goes particularly well with Crispy Chicken Fingers (page 23).

❶ Mix together the ingredients for the dressing in a small bowl.

❷ Place the sunflower seeds in a dry skillet and cook for a minute or so until they are a light golden brown color.

❸ Put the cabbage, carrot, apple, and scallion, if using, in a serving bowl. Add the sunflower seeds and mix until all the ingredients are combined.

❹ Spoon over the dressing and stir to coat the salad.

INGREDIENTS

2 tbsp sunflower seeds

½ small red cabbage, grated

1 large carrot, peeled and grated

½ apple, cored and diced

1 scallion, finely sliced (optional)

DRESSING

3 tbsp mayonnaise

1 tsp white wine vinegar, according to taste

2 tbsp plain yogurt

salt and freshly ground black pepper

Potato & Cabbage Patties

PREPARATION TIME *15 minutes* **COOKING TIME** *40 minutes*

FREEZING *suitable* **SERVES** *4 adults*

These cakes are a great way of getting children to eat cabbage!
They are delicious with a fresh tomato sauce and an egg on top.

❶ Cook the potatoes in salted boiling water for 15 minutes, or until tender. Drain well.

❷ Meanwhile, steam the cabbage for 5–8 minutes, or until tender.

❸ While the potatoes and cabbage are cooking, heat the oil in a heavy-bottomed skillet. Sauté the onion for 5–8 minutes.

❹ Place the potatoes and cabbage in a large bowl and mash using a potato masher. Add the onion, mustard, Cheddar cheese, egg, and seasoning and mix well with a wooden spoon until all the ingredients are combined. Leave to cool, or until the mixture is cool enough to handle.

INGREDIENTS
1 lb 9 oz/700 g potatoes, peeled and cut into even-sized pieces
4 cups Savoy or green cabbage, finely shredded
1 tbsp olive oil
1 onion, finely chopped
1 tsp Dijon mustard
¾ cup sharp Cheddar cheese, grated
1 egg, beaten
salt and freshly ground black pepper
flour, for dusting
vegetable oil, for sautéing

❺ Flour a large plate and your hands and shape the mixture into 8 patties. Heat enough oil to cover the base of a large heavy-bottomed skillet and sauté the patties over a medium heat for 3–4 minutes on each side.

Spicy Rice Balls with Tomato Sauce

PREPARATION TIME *15 minutes, plus 30 minutes cooling*
COOKING TIME *30 minutes* **FREEZING** *suitable* **SERVES** *4 adults*

These delicately spiced rice balls are similar to falafel but have a lighter texture. I've used risotto rice because its sticky texture helps the balls hold together, but any type of cooked rice is suitable. You can serve them wrapped in a warm tortilla with houmus, instead of the tomato sauce, if liked.

INGREDIENTS

½ cup risotto rice

1½ cups vegetable bouillon

1 tbsp olive oil

1 onion, finely chopped

2 cloves garlic, finely chopped

1 tsp ground cumin

1 tsp ground coriander

½ tsp paprika

1 cup canned garbanzo beans, drained and rinsed

1 egg, beaten

fine cornmeal or polenta, for coating

3–4 tbsp sesame seeds

sunflower oil, for sautéing

TOMATO SAUCE

1 tbsp olive oil

1 clove garlic, finely chopped

1 glass white wine, optional

2¼ cups strained tomatoes

2 tsp tomato paste

½ tsp sugar

salt and freshly ground black pepper

❶ Place the rice in a saucepan and cover with the bouillon, stirring well. Bring to a boil, then reduce the heat and simmer, covered, for 15–20 minutes, or until the water has been absorbed and the rice is tender. Remove from the heat and leave the saucepan to sit, covered, for 5 minutes. Drain well and allow to cool for 30 minutes.

❷ To make the tomato sauce, heat the oil in a heavy-bottomed saucepan and sauté the garlic for 1 minute, or until softened. Add the wine, if using, and cook over a high heat for a minute or so, until the alcohol has evaporated. Reduce the heat to medium, add the strained tomatoes, tomato paste, and sugar and cook for 15 minutes, or until the sauce has reduced and thickened. Season to taste and keep the sauce warm.

❸ Meanwhile, make the rice balls. Heat the olive oil in a heavy-bottomed skillet. Add the onion and cook for 5–7 minutes, or until softened. Add the garlic and spices and cook for 1 minute, stirring. Stir in the garbanzo beans and the beaten egg.

❹ Transfer the rice, garbanzo bean, egg, and onion mixture to a blender. Season to taste and process until thick and smooth.

❺ Cover a large plate with a layer of cornmeal and sprinkle over the sesame seeds. For each rice ball, take a walnut-sized amount of the rice mixture and form it into a ball, then roll it in the cornmeal and sesame seed mixture. Repeat until you have used all the rice mixture.

❻ Heat enough oil to cover the base of a skillet, then cook the rice balls for 4 minutes, turning occasionally, until crisp and golden. (You will have to cook the balls in batches.) Drain the rice balls on paper towels to mop up any excess oil.

❼ To serve, divide the tomato sauce between 4 shallow bowls, then arrange the rice balls on top.

Banana Custard Scrunch

PREPARATION TIME *5 minutes* **COOKING TIME** *3 minutes*

FREEZING *unsuitable* **SERVES** *4 adults*

Layers of honey-coated oats, bananas, and yogurt custard taste
indulgent, but couldn't be easier to make. Children love it when
the scrunch is served in tall glasses with a long spoon.

❶ Mix together the yogurt and
custard in a bowl.

❷ Put the oats in a dry skillet and
toast them for a minute. Add the
honey and stir to coat the oats.
Cook for 2 minutes over a
medium heat, stirring, until the
oats become golden and slightly
crisp at the edges.

❸ To serve, spoon the oat
mixture, reserving a little to

INGREDIENTS
¼ cup thick plain yogurt
scant 1 cup ready-made custard
¾ cup porridge oats
2 tbsp runny honey
2–3 bananas, sliced

decorate, into the bottom of
4 glasses or ramekins. Arrange
two-thirds of the banana over
the oats, then top with the yogurt
custard. Top with the reserved
bananas and sprinkle with oats.

Strawberry & Vanilla Yogurt Ice

PREPARATION TIME *20 minutes* **FREEZING** *suitable*

SERVES *4 adults*

Yogurt adds a refreshing tang to this homemade fresh fruit ice, which can be scooped into small cones—the perfect size for toddlers of this age. Live yogurt has a beneficial effect on the digestive system and can help to fight off stomach upsets. As an added bonus, this ice is free from additives and stabilizers.

❶ Whisk together the yogurt and mascarpone in a bowl. Pour into a shallow, freezer-proof container and freeze for 1 hour.

❷ Purée the strawberries and vanilla extract in a blender until smooth, then mix with the honey.

❸ Remove the semifrozen yogurt mixture from the freezer and fold in the strawberry and honey mixture. Beat well until smooth.

❹ Return the yogurt ice to the freezer and freeze for a further 2 hours. Remove from the freezer and beat again, then freeze until solid. Serve in scoops with fresh strawberries, if liked.

INGREDIENTS
1½ cups thick live plain yogurt
scant 1 cup mascarpone cheese
2 cups strawberries, hulled and sliced
1 tsp vanilla extract
6 tbsp runny honey

Baked Peach Crumbles

PREPARATION TIME *15 minutes*   **COOKING TIME** *30 minutes*

FREEZING *suitable*   **SERVES** *4 adults*

These individual crumbles are especially delicious with a good dollop of custard or ice cream. Plums and nectarines also work well.

INGREDIENTS
4 peaches, halved and pitted
⅓ cup all-purpose flour, sifted
2 tbsp butter, plus extra for greasing
2 tbsp porridge oats
3 tbsp brown sugar

❶ Preheat the oven to 350°F/180°C.

❷ Arrange the peach halves in the bottom of a small, lightly greased ovenproof dish.

VARIATION

Add 1 tbsp of chopped mixed nuts and 1 tbsp finely chopped dried dates to the crumble mixture.

❸ Put the flour and butter in a bowl and rub together with your fingertips to resemble coarse bread crumbs. Stir in the oats and sugar and mix well.

❹ Sprinkle generous amounts of the crumble mixture over the peach halves. Bake for 25–30 minutes, or until the peaches are tender and the crumble mixture is slightly crisp and golden.

Mini Chocolate & Banana Muffins

PREPARATION TIME *10 minutes*   **COOKING TIME** *15 minutes*
FREEZING *suitable*   **MAKES** *24 small muffins*

These muffins are a good size for toddlers and are extremely delicious, especially when warm and the chocolate is still gooey.

❶ Preheat the oven to 400°F/200°C. Butter 2 x 12-hole small muffin pans.

❷ Sift together the flour, salt, and baking powder in a large bowl. Add the sugar and chocolate to the flour mixture and then stir.

❸ Place the milk, eggs, butter, and yogurt in a separate bowl and whisk until combined. Add the egg mixture to the flour mixture, stirring until just combined, but don't overmix or it will result in heavy muffins.

❹ Gently fold the mashed bananas into the mixture.

INGREDIENTS
¼ cup all-purpose flour
pinch of salt
1 tsp baking powder
¾ cup brown sugar
4 oz/115 g sweet chocolate, broken into chunks
3 tbsp milk
2 eggs, beaten
generous ½ cup sweet butter, melted
3 tbsp low-fat plain yogurt
2 small bananas, mashed

❺ Spoon the mixture into the greased muffin pans and bake for 12–15 minutes, or until risen and slightly golden. Leave in the tin for 5 minutes, then turn out on to a wire rack to cool.

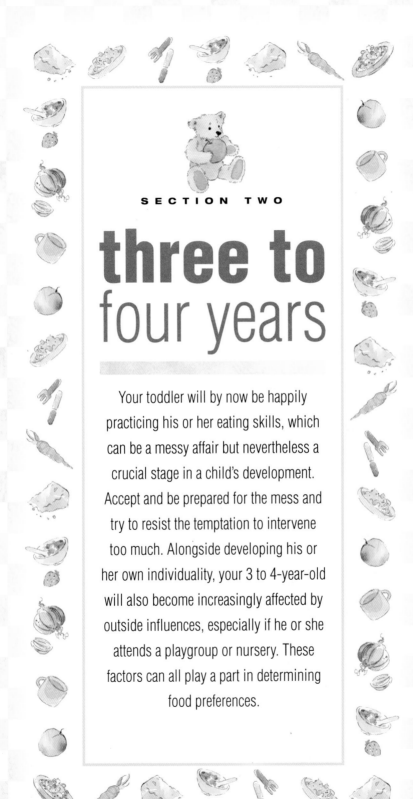

SECTION TWO

three to
four years

Your toddler will by now be happily practicing his or her eating skills, which can be a messy affair but nevertheless a crucial stage in a child's development. Accept and be prepared for the mess and try to resist the temptation to intervene too much. Alongside developing his or her own individuality, your 3 to 4-year-old will also become increasingly affected by outside influences, especially if he or she attends a playgroup or nursery. These factors can all play a part in determining food preferences.

Nutritional Needs

The nutritional requirements of 3 to 4-year-olds are not that different from those of an 18-month-old. Although by this age the rate of growth has slowed down considerably, 3 to 4-year-olds are generally more active and their diets need to compensate for this increase in energy levels. High-energy foods still need to be included in your toddler's diet.

All small children require sufficient calories and a variety of foods (based on the major food groups mentioned on pages 6–9) to enable them to fuel high energy levels. They also need to be encouraged to enjoy the pleasures of eating and good food. This sounds simple in theory but good intentions can backfire in practice (see "Coping with a fussy eater"). Do stick to your guns, however, and rest assured that by providing plenty of fresh, unprocessed foods you are doing the best for your child's health and development in the long term. Nutritionists suggest that a varied, healthy diet can help to curb the major diseases that plague us in the West later in life, and there is also evidence to show that a good diet can help to relieve the symptoms of asthma.

OUTSIDE INFLUENCES

Many 3 to 4-year-olds attend a playgroup or nursery and this comes with its own challenges. You may be fortunate to find an ideal establishment that serves a

BELOW *Your child's likes and dislikes may be influenced by the nursery food that is offered.*

variety of freshly prepared, nutritious lunches, snacks, and healthy drinks. Realistically, food standards tend to vary and it can be awkward for parents to ask for changes without appearing difficult and demanding. Many nurseries are open to parents providing their own drinks, snacks, and packed lunches, and this may be a welcome option. Alternatively, take the softly-softly approach, arming yourself with relevant information, articles, and books. Often a lack of knowledge is to blame for poor food quality and all that is needed is a gentle nudge and a little encouragement.

EATING OUT

It can be a challenge to find a restaurant that not only welcomes children with open arms but also provides decent, healthy food. Most children's menus offer the usual repertoire of fish fingers and fries, burger and fries, and sausage and fries,

ABOVE *Eating out with a young child is a valuable experience and can be enjoyed by the whole family.*

followed by poor-quality ice cream and jello. There is also the further lure of a free gift! Consequently, all your good intentions fly out of the window.

Most children love the novelty of eating out and, from experience, the better quality pizza chains, Italian, Indian, and Chinese restaurants offer the best choice, and are often more welcoming to young children. Alternatively, choose a starter from the main menu or ask for a separate plate and share your meal. Sometimes the chef may provide a small child-sized portion of a main course.

Eating out can be a hit-or-miss affair, and it is best to pick a time when your little one is not very tired, or choose a restaurant that appears too formal, where it may be difficult to relax. To prevent occasional boredom, take along pens and paper or a small toy.

Coping With a Fussy Eater

All toddlers go through stages of picky eating and their appetites can be equally unpredictable. However frustrating this may be, try not to let this trouble you. There are plenty of stories of toddlers surviving on nothing but toast and jelly for some unimaginable amount of time—remarkably, most don't seem to suffer adverse effects.

How do you encourage your child to eat what you want him or her to eat, and what do you do if he or she refuses to eat at all? There are no easy answers, but the following guidelines should help you to cope easily with those challenging times:

• Don't force your child to eat. Conflict and tension serve only to make the situation worse and may lead to your child using mealtimes as a way of seeking attention. Children are remarkably clever at picking up on the anxieties of their parents and may well pick up on your own insecurities about food. Instead, try to coax gently or encourage your child to try a little bit of what you have prepared. I've found that my daughter will happily eat a meal once I've encouraged her to try "just a mouthful."

• If your gentle coaxing doesn't work, remove the food without making a fuss, but don't offer an alternative dish, however hard this may be. I know, speaking as someone who has prepared numerous alternatives when my daughter has refused to eat, that this is a losing battle. Your child is unlikely to starve and it's important that they learn to eat what's on offer, rather than expect endless alternatives.

• Don't overload your child's plate. Small amounts of food tend to be more acceptable.

• Praise and encourage your child as much as possible, even if they eat only a mouthful.

• Make eating fun. Picnics, even if it's only a cloth arranged on the kitchen floor, games, or basing a meal on a theme, such as a favorite cartoon character, book, or season, can be a real success.

• Try to ignore poor eating habits and complaints such as "yuck," however hard this may be.

• Ask a friend of your child's, who you know to be a good eater, to come to tea. Children learn by example and may be encouraged to eat by their peers. Beware, this can sometimes backfire—my daughter hasn't eaten peas since a friend said she disliked them!

ABOVE *Presenting small portions of food to your toddler is less off-putting and seems more manageable.*

• Don't fall into the trap of bribing your child with a dessert, and then giving it even if the main meal remains uneaten. This will only help to discourage good eating habits.

• Compromise is sometimes the only way to get your child to eat certain things. Combine foods that you know your child likes with others that are untried or previously rejected.

MEAL PLANNER 2

3-4 YEARS	BREAKFAST	LUNCH
Day 1	Diced bacon & broiled tomatoes Toast, yogurt	Pasta bolognese, broccoli Fruit salad
Day 2	Porridge, fruit, toast	Frittata, coleslaw Baked apple and custard
Day 3	Cereal/muesli, muffin	Creamy tomato & lentil soup Garlic bread with cheese Mini chocolate & banana mu
Day 4	Poached egg & beans Toast Yogurt	Higgledy-piggledy pie, potatoes and vegetables Ice cream sundae
Day 5	Cereal, toast	Starfish pie with green bean Fruity chocolate bread puddi
Day 6	Pancake with stewed apple Yogurt	Pork & apple casserole Potatoes & vegetables Baked peach crumbles
Day 7	Cheese scrambled eggs on toast Fruit	Winter sausage hot pot Vegetables Sandcastle cakes

TEA	SUPPER
Paella Ice cream sundae	Guacamole with tortilla pita bread Vegetable sticks Fruit & milky drink
Chinese noodles Banana custard scrunch	Tortilla parcels Fruit & milky drink
Golden fish fingers & potato wedges with peas Strawberry & vanilla yogurt ice	Sardines on toast Fruit & milky drink
Chicken sticks, coleslaw Baked potato Plain yogurt & fruit	Cheese on toast Fruit & milky drink
Spicy rice balls with tomato sauce, vegetables Yogurt	Sandwich Fruit & milky drink
Creamy smoked salmon & broccoli pasta Flapjack	Houmus/cheese tortilla Vegetable sticks Fruit & milky drink
Baked potato with pesto & cheese Buttermilk pancakes with hot maple bananas	Raisin & pecan muffins Fruit & milky drink

Creamy Tomato & Lentil Soup

PREPARATION TIME *10 minutes* **COOKING TIME** *45 minutes*
FREEZING *suitable* **SERVES** *4 adults*

Remarkably, children who turn their noses up at vegetables will happily eat them when liquidized into a soup. Most toddlers love tomato soup, and this one is free from the additives often found in manufactured alternatives. The lentils add extra goodness and substance, but they can be swapped for beans or cooked rice. I usually serve this soup with mini cheese toasts, although croûtons, garlic bread, or a hunk of crusty bread are just as good.

INGREDIENTS

¼ cup split red lentils, rinsed

1 tbsp olive oil

1 onion, chopped

1 carrot, peeled and finely chopped

1 celery stick, chopped

1 lb 2 oz/500 g carton creamed tomatoes

2½ cups vegetable bouillon

cream or plain yogurt, to serve (optional)

salt and freshly ground black pepper

CHEESE TOASTS

8 slices French bread

butter, for spreading

½ cup Gruyère or sharp Cheddar cheese, grated

½ tsp dried oregano

❶ Place the lentils in a saucepan, cover with water, and bring to a boil. Reduce the heat and simmer, half covered, for 25 minutes, or until tender. Drain the lentils well and set aside.

❷ While the lentils are cooking, make the soup. Heat the oil in a heavy-bottomed saucepan. Add the onion, cover the pan and sweat for 10 minutes, or until softened. Add the carrot and celery and sweat for a further 2 minutes, stirring occasionally to prevent the vegetables sticking to the bottom of the pan.

❸ Add the creamed tomatoes and bouillon and bring to a boil. Reduce the heat and simmer, half covered, for 25 minutes, or until the vegetables are tender and the liquid has reduced and thickened. Add the lentils to the pan.

❹ Carefully pour the mixture into a blender and blend until smooth and creamy. Return the soup to the pan, season to taste and heat through if necessary. Swirl a spoonful of cream, if using, over the soup and serve.

❺ For the cheese toasts, preheat the broiler to high. Lightly toast the French bread on one side. Butter the untoasted side and sprinkle with the Gruyère cheese and oregano. Broil until golden.

Golden Fish Fingers with Sweet Potato Wedges

PREPARATION TIME *15 minutes* **COOKING TIME** *35 minutes*

FREEZING *suitable* **MAKES** *8–10 fingers*

If making your own fish fingers sounds like too much effort, this simple, quick version may change your mind, and you can also guarantee the quality of the ingredients used. The cod fillets are covered in a crisp, golden crumb, made from fresh bread crumbs, and I like to serve them with sweet potato wedges.

❶ Preheat the oven to 400°F/200°C.

❷ Dry the sweet potato wedges on a clean dish cloth. Place the oil in a roasting pan and heat for a few minutes in the oven. Arrange the potatoes in the pan and bake for 30–35 minutes, turning them halfway through, until tender and golden.

❸ Meanwhile, cut the cod into strips, about ¾ in/2 cm wide.

❹ Season the flour and add the paprika. Roll the cod strips in the seasoned flour until coated, shaking off any excess, then dip them in the beaten egg. Roll the cod strips in the bread crumbs until evenly coated.

❺ Heat enough oil to cover the base of a large, non-stick skillet. Carefully arrange the fish fingers in the pan—you may have to cook them in batches—and cook them for 3–4 minutes on each side, or until crisp and golden. Drain on paper towels before serving, if necessary.

❻ Serve the fish fingers with the sweet potato wedges and peas.

INGREDIENTS

10 oz/280 g thick cod fillets, skin and bones removed

flour, for dusting

1 tsp paprika

1 egg, beaten

fresh bread crumbs or fine cornmeal, for coating

sunflower oil, for sautéing

salt and freshly ground black pepper

SWEET POTATO WEDGES

2 medium sweet potatoes, scrubbed and cut into wedges

1 tbsp olive oil

Surf 'n' Turf Paella

PREPARATION TIME *15 minutes*   **COOKING TIME** *30 minutes*

FREEZING *suitable*   **SERVES** *2–3 adults*

This golden rice dish is infused with saffron, but you can use turmeric instead, which gives a similar sunshine color. Paella rice is perfect for young children as it has a tender, melt-in-the-mouth texture when cooked.

❶ Heat the oil in a large heavy-bottomed sauté pan (with a lid). Add the onion and cook for 5 minutes, or until softened. Add the chicken breast, bell pepper, and garlic and sauté for 5 minutes over a medium heat, stirring the mixture frequently.

❷ Add the tomato, tomato paste, saffron, and bouillon to the pan. Stir in the rice and bring to a boil, then reduce the heat. Simmer the rice, covered, for 15 minutes, or until the rice is tender.

❸ Add the peas, shrimp, and seasoning and cook for a further 2–3 minutes, or until the shrimp have heated through.

INGREDIENTS

2 tbsp olive oil

1 onion, diced

2 skinless chicken breasts, sliced

1 small red bell pepper, seeded and diced

2 cloves garlic, chopped

1 tomato, seeded and chopped

1 tbsp tomato paste

pinch of saffron

2½ cups hot chicken or vegetable bouillon

generous 1 cup paella rice

½ cup frozen peas

4 oz/115 g cooked shrimp, thawed if frozen

salt and freshly ground black pepper

Pasta Bolognese

PREPARATION TIME *10 minutes*   **COOKING TIME** *30 minutes*

FREEZING *suitable*   **SERVES** *4 adults*

Spaghetti is a real favorite with toddlers, who love the slurping and the accompanying mess—so be prepared! Vegetarians can opt for soy or Quorn instead of ground meat. Use good-quality meat if opting for the non-vegetarian version.

❶ Heat the oil in a heavy-bottomed, non-stick saucepan. Add the onion and sauté, half covered, for 5 minutes, or until softened. Add the garlic, carrot, and mushrooms, if using, and sauté for a further 3 minutes, stirring well.

INGREDIENTS

3 cups spaghetti or pasta of your choice

BOLOGNESE SAUCE

2 tbsp olive oil

1 onion, finely chopped

2 cloves garlic, finely chopped

1 carrot, peeled and finely chopped

generous 1 cup mushrooms, peeled and sliced or chopped (optional)

1 tsp dried oregano

½ tsp dried thyme

1 bay leaf

10 oz/280 g lean ground meat

1 glass white wine (optional)

1¼ cups bouillon

1¼ cups strained tomatoes

salt and freshly ground black pepper

2 Add the herbs and meat to the pan and cook until the meat has browned, stirring regularly.

3 Add the wine, if using, and cook over a high heat until the alcohol has evaporated, then add the bouillon and strained tomatoes. Reduce the heat, season and cook over a medium heat, half covered, for 15–20 minutes, or until the sauce has reduced and thickened. Remove the bay leaf.

4 Meanwhile, cook the pasta according to the instructions on the package, until the pasta is tender. Drain well and mix together the pasta and sauce.

Bacon, Pea, & Potato Frittata

PREPARATION TIME *15 minutes* **COOKING TIME** *20 minutes*

FREEZING *unsuitable* **SERVES** *3–4 adults*

This frittata is similar to the Spanish tortilla. Serve it cut into wedges or fingers, with crusty bread and green vegetables or a salad. This is a good food for small fingers to handle.

❶ Preheat the broiler to high. Broil the bacon until crisp. Allow to cool slightly, then cut into small pieces and set aside.

❷ Heat the oil in a large heavy-bottomed, ovenproof skillet, add the onion and sauté for 5 minutes, or until softened and tender, stirring occasionally.

INGREDIENTS

2–3 slices good-quality bacon

1½ tbsp olive oil

1 small onion, finely chopped

12 oz/350 g new potatoes, cooked, halved or quartered, if large

½ cup frozen baby peas

6 free range eggs, lightly beaten

salt and freshly ground black pepper

❸ Add the potatoes and cook for a further 5 minutes, or until golden, stirring to prevent them sticking to the pan. Add the bacon pieces and peas, and spread the mixture evenly over the base of the pan.

❹ Reheat the broiler to high. Season the beaten eggs, then pour them over the onion and potato mixture. Cook over a moderate heat for 5–6 minutes, or until the eggs are just set and the base of the frittata is lightly golden.

❺ Place the pan under the broiler and cook the top for 3 minutes, or until set and lightly golden. Serve the frittata warm or cold, cut into wedges or fingers.

Chinese Noodles

PREPARATION TIME *10 minutes, plus 1 hour marinating*
COOKING TIME *20 minutes* **FREEZING** *unsuitable* **SERVES** *4 adults*

Toddlers seem to love noodles as much as pasta and this stir-fry is no exception. I've chosen brightly colored vegetables for maximum appeal, but experiment with different types. Whatever you choose, they are at their best when still slightly crunchy.

❶ Mix together the ingredients for the marinade in a shallow dish. Add the bean curd and spoon the marinade over. Refrigerate for 1 hour to marinate, turning the bean curd to allow the flavors to infuse.

❷ Preheat the oven to 400°F/200°C. Using a slotted spoon, remove the bean curd from the marinade and reserve the liquid. Arrange the bean curd on a cookie sheet and roast for 20 minutes, turning occasionally,

INGREDIENTS

2 generous cups medium egg noodles

1 block of bean curd, cubed

1 tbsp peanut or vegetable oil

1 red bell pepper, seeded and sliced

8 oz/225 g broccoli florets

6 oz/175 g baby corn, halved
lengthwise

2–3 tbsp water

2 scallions, finely sliced

1 tbsp sesame seeds,
toasted (optional)

MARINADE

1 clove garlic, finely chopped

1 in/2.5 cm piece fresh root ginger,
peeled and grated

1 tsp sesame oil

1 tbsp runny honey

2 tbsp dark soy sauce

until the bean curd is golden and crisp on all sides.

❸ Meanwhile, cook the noodles in plenty of salted boiling water according to the instructions on the package, until the noodles are tender, then drain. Rinse the noodles under cold running water and drain again.

❹ Heat a wok or heavy-bottomed skillet, then add the oil. Add the bell pepper, broccoli, and corn and cook, tossing and stirring continuously, over a medium-high heat for 5–8 minutes, or until the vegetables have softened. Add the water and continue to cook until the vegetables are just tender, but remain slightly crunchy.

❺ Stir in the marinade, noodles, bean curd, and scallions and cook until heated through, tossing to coat them in the liquid.

❻ Serve sprinkled with the sesame seeds, if using.

Winter Sausage Hot Pot

PREPARATION TIME *15 minutes* **COOKING TIME** *45 minutes*
FREEZING *suitable* **SERVES** *4 adults*

A satisfying, warming stew, which has a savory scone topping and can be made with either pork or vegetarian sausages. The alcohol in the wine will evaporate during cooking.

❶ Preheat the broiler to high. Broil the sausages, turning them occasionally, until they are cooked and golden. Set aside.

❷ Preheat the oven to 400°F/200°C.

❸ Meanwhile, heat the oil in a heavy-bottomed saucepan and sauté the onion, covered, for 5 minutes, or until softened. Add the garlic, celery, bell pepper, zucchini, and herbs and sauté, covered, for a further 5 minutes.

❹ Add the wine, if using, and cook over a medium-high heat for a few minutes until the alcohol has evaporated. If using

7 Gradually stir in the milk using a spatula and form the mixture into a dough with your floured hands. Knead lightly on a floured counter until smooth. Take walnut-sized pieces of the dough and roll them into balls. Flatten them and arrange them in a circle on the top of the hot pot.

8 Brush the top of the scones with milk and bake for 20 minutes, or until the scones have risen and are golden.

INGREDIENTS
6 pork or vegetarian sausages
1 tbsp olive oil
1 onion, chopped
1 clove garlic, chopped
1 celery stick, finely chopped
1 red bell pepper, seeded and diced
2 zucchini, sliced
2 tsp chopped fresh rosemary
1 tsp thyme
1 bay leaf
1 glass of white wine (optional)
⅔–¾ cup vegetable bouillon
1½ cups strained tomatoes
½ tsp sugar
14-oz/400-g can borlotti beans, drained and rinsed

the wine, add the smaller amount of bouillon; if not, opt for the greater quantity. Reduce the heat to medium, stir, and add the strained tomatoes and sugar. Stir again and cook for 10 minutes, or until the sauce has reduced and begins to thicken.

5 Slice the cooked sausages and add them to the sauce with the beans. Stir and spoon the mixture into a casserole dish.

6 To make the scone topping, place the flour, salt, and baking powder into a bowl and mix. Add the margarine and rub with your fingertips until the mixture resembles bread crumbs.

SCONE TOPPING
1¼ cups self-rising flour, sifted
½ tsp salt
1 heaped tsp baking powder
3 tbsp butter or margarine
¼–⅓ cup milk, plus extra for glazing

Higgledy-Piggledy Pie

PREPARATION TIME *20 minutes, plus 30 minutes resting*
COOKING TIME *55 minutes* **FREEZING** *suitable* **SERVES** *4 adults*

This free-form pie encases a rich tomato, eggplant, and kidney bean filling. If your pie dough cracks, just patch it up—it adds to the pie's rustic charm. The pie dough is enriched with Parmesan cheese, but this can be omitted if desired.

❶ Preheat the oven to 425°F/220°C. For the pie dough, rub together the all-purpose and whole-wheat flours, salt, and butter until the mixture resembles fine bread crumbs, then stir in the Parmesan cheese.

❷ Add enough cold water to form a dough, then turn out the dough on to a lightly floured counter and knead lightly to form a smooth and elastic dough. Wrap in plastic wrap and chill for 30 minutes.

INGREDIENTS

1 medium eggplant, cubed

1 red bell pepper, seeded and diced

2 tbsp olive oil

1 onion, finely chopped

1 zucchini, sliced

2 cloves garlic, crushed

1 tsp dried oregano

1½ cups canned red kidney beans, drained and rinsed

salt and freshly ground black pepper

2 cups chopped tomatoes

2 tbsp cream of wheat

½ cup Cheddar cheese, grated

1 egg, beaten

PIE DOUGH

1 cup all-purpose flour

1 cup whole-wheat flour

1 cup butter or vegetable margarine

⅔ cup Parmesan cheese, finely grated

❸ To make the filling, sprinkle the eggplant with salt and leave for 30 minutes to remove any bitter juices. Rinse and pat dry with paper towels.

❹ Heat the oil in a large heavy-bottomed skillet. Cook the onions for 5 minutes, or until softened. Add the bell pepper and eggplant and cook for 5 minutes, or until tender, then add the zucchini, garlic, and oregano. Cook for a further 5 minutes. Add the kidney beans, seasoning, and chopped tomatoes. Cook for 8 minutes, or until the sauce has reduced, then set aside to cool.

❺ Divide the pie dough into four pieces and roll out on a lightly floured counter to form equal-sized rounds. Place on a lightly greased cookie sheet. Brush with a little of the beaten egg and sprinkle over the cream of wheat, leaving a 1½-in/4-cm border. Spoon over the filling, leaving a border, and sprinkle with the Cheddar cheese.

❻ Gather up the edges of the pie dough to partly cover the filling—the pie should remain open in the middle. Brush with the remaining egg and bake for 25–30 minutes, or until golden.

Tortilla Parcels

PREPARATION TIME *5 minutes*   **COOKING TIME** *2 minutes*
FREEZING *unsuitable*   **MAKES** *2 parcels*

Soft, floury tortillas make a perfect snack or light lunch. These are filled with tuna, mozzarella cheese, and diced tomato, but you could vary the filling according to likes and dislikes. Guacamole or houmus are also popular with children.

❶ Place the mozzarella cheese, tuna, tomato, and seasoning along the center of the tortilla. Fold in the sides, then the ends of the tortilla to encase the filling.

❷ Place the parcel, seam-side down, in a dry, non-stick skillet and gently warm over a low-medium heat for 2 minutes, turning once, until the tortilla is lightly golden and the filling is warmed through. Cut the tortilla in half and serve immediately.

INGREDIENTS

4 slices of mozzarella cheese, drained and dried with paper towels

2 tbsp canned tuna in oil, drained and mashed

1 small tomato, seeded and diced

1 soft tortilla

salt and freshly ground black pepper

Ice Cream Strawberry Sundae

PREPARATION TIME *10 minutes* **COOKING TIME** *12 minutes*

FREEZING *sauce can be frozen* **SERVES** *4*

This sumptuous dessert is a real treat, and is enjoyed by adults and children alike! Strawberries are particularly popular with toddlers, and they are sweet enough not to need much extra sugar. Be sure to use good-quality dairy ice cream.

❶ To make the sauce, process the strawberries with the orange juice in a blender until smooth. Transfer the mixture to a saucepan and add the sugar. Cook over a medium heat for 10–12 minutes, or until thickened. Leave to cool.

❷ To serve, place a spoonful of the strawberry sauce in the bottom of a tall glass. Add two scoops of ice cream and another spoonful of fruit sauce. Sprinkle with the nuts and chocolate. Arrange the marshmallows on top. Repeat for four sundaes.

INGREDIENTS

8 scoops of good-quality vanilla ice cream

¼ cup chopped mixed nuts, lightly toasted in a dry skillet

grated chocolate and marshmallows, to serve

STRAWBERRY SAUCE

2 generous cups strawberries, hulled and halved

2 tbsp freshly squeezed orange juice

2 tbsp superfine sugar

VARIATION

Replace the strawberry sauce with a rich chocolate sauce. Melt 3½ oz/100 g of good-quality milk chocolate in a bowl, placed over a pan of simmering water. (Make sure the bowl does not touch the water.) Stir very occasionally until melted. Heat 2 tbsp milk, ¼ cup heavy cream, and 2 tbsp superfine sugar in a small saucepan and bring to the boil. Gently pour the mixture on to the melted chocolate and whisk until combined and smooth. Serve warm.

Fruity Chocolate Bread Pudding

PREPARATION TIME *15 minutes* **COOKING TIME** *35 minutes*
FREEZING *suitable* **SERVES** *4 adults*

A rich, comforting dessert that just melts in the mouth. It is made with fruit bread, but ordinary sliced bread, muffins, brioche, or panettone work just as well. Toddlers love it with custard.

❶ Preheat the oven to 400°F/200°C. Butter a 10 x 8-in/25 x 20-cm baking dish. Arrange half the fruit bread in the dish in a single layer.

❷ Spread the remaining fruit bread with the chocolate spread. Arrange another layer of fruit bread over the chocolate bread, making sure that it lies flat.

❸ Gently heat the milk and vanilla extract in a saucepan, until it just reaches boiling point. Remove from the heat and whisk in the egg and maple syrup, mixing well.

❹ Pour the egg mixture over the fruit, lightly pressing down the bread so it is submerged. Leave to soak for 10 minutes.

❺ Bake for 25–30 minutes, or until set and golden. To serve, cut into 4 portions and sprinkle the top of the pudding with ground cinnamon.

INGREDIENTS

9½ oz/275 g sliced fruit bread, crusts removed

6 tbsp good-quality chocolate spread

1¼ cups milk

½ tsp vanilla extract

1 large free-range egg, beaten

1 tbsp maple syrup

ground cinnamon, for decorating

Buttermilk Pancakes with Hot Maple Bananas

PREPARATION TIME *5 minutes* **COOKING TIME** *5 minutes*

FREEZING *pancakes suitable* **SERVES** *4 adults*

A simple and very quick pudding-cum-breakfast that nevertheless tastes delicious. Serve the pancakes with a spoonful of plain yogurt or vanilla ice cream.

❶ To make the pancakes, place the flour, salt, sugar, and baking powder in a large bowl and mix everything together well.

❷ Mix together the beaten egg, buttermilk, and melted butter, then add it to the flour mixture and beat well to remove any lumps. (This makes a thick batter.)

❸ Heat a teaspoon of the oil in a heavy-bottomed skillet. Place heaped tablespoons of the batter in the pan and flatten with the back of a spoon. Cook for 3 minutes, or until set and golden, then turn over and cook the other side of the pancake for 2 minutes. Cover with foil and keep warm in an ovenproof dish placed in a preheated oven. Make the remaining pancakes.

❹ Melt the butter in a heavy-bottomed skillet. Add the bananas and cook for 1 minute over a medium heat, turning once to coat them in the butter.

❺ Add the maple syrup and cook the bananas for a further 1–2 minutes. Spoon over the pancakes, to serve.

INGREDIENTS
3 tbsp sweet butter
4 bananas, thickly sliced diagonally
6 tbsp maple syrup
1 tbsp flaked almonds, toasted (optional)

PANCAKES
1¼ cups all-purpose flour, sifted
pinch of salt
2 tbsp superfine sugar
1 tsp baking powder
1 egg, beaten
284 ml carton buttermilk
2 tbsp butter, melted
sunflower oil, for frying

Sandcastle Cakes

PREPARATION TIME *10 minutes* **COOKING TIME** *20 minutes*
FREEZING *unsuitable* **MAKES** *4 cakes*

These fun, decorated sponge cakes are great for parties or a special teatime treat when your children have been extra good! Top the cakes with homemade flags with each child's name on it for an added fun factor.

❶ Preheat the oven to 435°F/180°C. Lightly grease 4 dariole moulds and line the base with a circle of waxed paper.

❷ Sift the flour into a large mixing bowl. Add the sugar, butter, and eggs and beat together until smooth and creamy.

❸ Divide the mixture between the moulds, filling them three-quarters full. Place on a cookie sheet and cook for 20 minutes, or until risen and golden. Leave for 5 minutes, then turn out on to a wire rack to cool.

❹ Trim the base of each cake so that it stands up. Heat the jam in a small saucepan until runny, then brush it over the top and sides of the cakes. Roll the cakes in the hundreds and thousands and decorate with the silver balls.

INGREDIENTS

1 cup self-rising flour

generous ½ cup superfine sugar

½ cup butter or margarine, plus extra for greasing

2 eggs

3 tbsp strawberry jam

silver balls and hundreds and thousands, to decorate

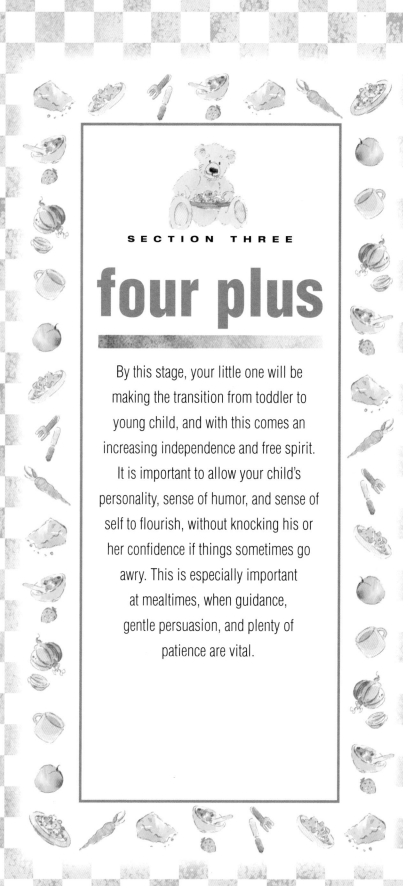

SECTION THREE

four plus

By this stage, your little one will be
making the transition from toddler to
young child, and with this comes an
increasing independence and free spirit.
It is important to allow your child's
personality, sense of humor, and sense of
self to flourish, without knocking his or
her confidence if things sometimes go
awry. This is especially important
at mealtimes, when guidance,
gentle persuasion, and plenty of
patience are vital.

Nutritional Needs

For many young children, their fourth year heralds the start of full-time education. School presents its own challenges and it can be a time when good intentions and eating habits fall by the wayside. However, a nutritious, varied diet is an important as ever—sustaining and boosting energy levels, concentration and, some experts say, even brain power.

Many children do not eat breakfast before they go to school or simply rely on a bag of potato chips or a candy bar to fight off hunger pangs until lunchtime. Many nutritionists believe that breakfast is the most important meal of the day, replenishing nutrients and energy stocks depleted overnight. High-carbohydrate foods such as low-sugar breakfast cereals, bread, and beans provide sustained energy and help to keep blood sugar levels on an even keel. Recent research suggests that children who eat a carbohydrate-based breakfast are likely to perform better at school.

School lunches vary in quality and choice depending on where you live. A packed lunch may be the only way you can ensure that your child is getting a nutritious variety of foods—that's as long as it's eaten! Turn to page 77 for some ideas. At this age, tea or supper may become the main meal of the day. Even if your child has a cooked school lunch, it's advisable to give him or her a decent meal in the afternoon or evening to ensure that he or she is getting a sufficient range of nutrients. Now your child is older, it may be feasible to eat communal meals. Eating together encourages children to try a wider variety of food as well as to enjoy the social aspect of sharing mealtimes.

JUNK FOODS

There are very few completely "bad" foods, but there are many which are best avoided—those containing E numbers and other additives, artificial colorings, sweeteners, hydrogenated and saturated fat, as well as excessively sugary and salty foods. Poor-quality foods, including cheap cookies, cakes, processed meats and cheeses, pies, sugary fizzy drinks, and packet desserts are just some of

ABOVE *A good breakfast before a day at school is vital to keep energy levels high, and stops your child snacking.*

the foods that fall into this category. If finances allow, it is really worth buying healthier alternatives, which are usually made with superior ingredients and fewer additives.

We all buy convenience foods, some more than others, but try to opt for fish fingers containing the highest percentage of fish, sausages and pies with a high meat content, jam with a high fruit content, and cookies, cakes, and cereals that are lower in sugar than some of their counterparts. Better still, it really is worth taking the time to make your own versions.

• To make healthier French fries: cut potatoes into wedges, keeping the skin, then brush with olive oil and bake in the oven. A good source of vitamin C and fiber.

• Top a pizza base with homemade tomato sauce, grated cheese, and vegetables. A good source of vitamin C, beta-carotene, and calcium.

• Use lean meat and grated vegetables to make homemade burgers. Combine mashed beans and grated vegetables to make a vegetarian alternative. Brush with oil and broil. A good source of iron, and vitamins C and B.

• Make a healthier version of a "knickerbocker glory" with plain yogurt or good-quality ice cream, fresh fruit purée, and chopped toasted nuts. Pile high in a glass. A good source of vitamins B and C, and calcium.

M E A L   P L A N N E R   3

4+ YEARS	BREAKFAST	LUNCH
Day 1	Porridge and dried apricots Toast	Noodle soup with chicken/ bean curd/prawns Plain yogurt OR packed/school lunch
Day 2	Hard-cooked egg, toast, banana	Chicken, apple, & nut salad, bread Baked apple & custard OR packed/school lunch
Day 3	Cereal, toasted fruit bread	Chinese omelet roll, yogurt OR packed/school lunch
Day 4	Toasted bacon and tomato sandwich, yogurt	Hearty bean & pasta soup Tortilla parcel Strawberry & vanilla yogurt ice OR packed/school lunch
Day 5	Cereal, toast, melon	Creamy smoked salmon & broccoli Fresh fruit sticks OR packed/school lunch
Day 6	Potato & cabbage patties Broiled tomatoes Fresh orange juice	Spicy rice balls with tomato sauce Chicken fingers Ice cream sundae
Day 7	Scrambled egg Kipper & toast	Thanksgiving pie Roast potatoes and vegetables Little Jack Horner pudding

TEA	SUPPER
Sunny rice, green vegetables Pancakes with maple bananas	Sandwich, fruit Milky drink
Green giant pasta Garlic bread Sandcastle cakes	Muffin/biscuit Fruit Milky drink
Honey salmon kebabs, rice and vegetables Passion cake squares	Crackers and cheese Apple and grapes Milky drink
Baby burger Sweet potato wedges Grated carrot Baked peach crumbles	Sardines on toast Fruit Milky drink
Winter sausage hot pot, vegetables Plain yogurt	Gingerbread person Fruit Milky drink
Pork & apple casserole Potatoes and vegetables Fruity chocolate bread pudding	Malt loaf Fruit Milky drink
Creamy tomato & lentil soup Pizza fingers Banana custard scrunch	Sandwich Fruit Milky drink

Lunchbox Ideas

Many of us get stuck in a rut when it comes to providing interesting and varied lunchboxes everyday—it's all too easy to stick to the usual sandwich, crisps, yogurt, and apple. Time is also at a premium in the morning, when preparing a lunchbox has to be juggled with breakfast, getting dressed, and the school run. The following ideas will hopefully inspire and most can be prepared ahead of time, so they shouldn't demand too much attention when time is against you. By varying your daily offering, you add an element of surprise and hopefully your efforts will pay off—there's nothing more frustrating than when a lunchbox returns home with its contents untouched.

Mini Pasties

PREPARATION TIME *10 minutes, plus 15 minutes soaking*

COOKING TIME *35 minutes* **FREEZING** *suitable* **MAKES** 6

These mini pasties make a great addition to a lunchbox or picnic and are the right size for toddlers to hold. They can also be served warm for supper with new potatoes and vegetables. The flaky puff-pie-dough triangles encase a mixture of soy mince (or lean ground beef) and vegetables—make plenty, they'll go quickly!

❶ Put the soy mince in a bowl and cover with boiling water. Add the yeast extract and stir until dissolved. Leave the mince for 15 minutes, until rehydrated. Meanwhile, steam or boil the potatoes and carrots until tender.

❷ Heat the oil in a pan and sauté the onion for 5 minutes. Add the garlic and sauté for a further minute, stirring occasionally, until the onion has softened.

❸ Add the cooked carrot and potato, parsley, soy mince (and any soaking liquid), strained tomatoes, and soy sauce to the pan. Stir thoroughly, season with pepper to taste, and cook for 10 minutes, or until it is quite dry.

❹ Preheat the oven to 400°F/200°C. Place the pie dough on a counter and cut into 4-in/6 x 10-cm squares. Place a heaped teaspoon of the filling in the

INGREDIENTS

1 oz/25 g dried soy mince
(look for one that is GM free)

½ tsp yeast extract

1 small potato, peeled and diced

1 small carrot, peeled and diced

1 tsp vegetable oil

1 small onion, finely chopped

1 clove garlic, crushed

1 tbsp finely chopped fresh parsley

2 tbsp strained tomatoes

1 tbsp soy sauce

freshly ground black pepper

13 oz/375 g ready-rolled puff pie dough,
thawed if frozen

1 egg, beaten, to glaze

center of each pie dough square. Brush the edges with the beaten egg and fold the pie dough in half to make a triangle. Seal the edges with a fork, then repeat to make 5 more pasties.

❺ Place the pasties on a lightly greased cookie sheet, brush with the remaining egg and make a small air hole in the top using a toothpick. Bake for 15–20 minutes, or until risen.

Guacamole

PREPARATION TIME *5 minutes* **FREEZING** *unsuitable* **SERVES** *2–4*

This creamy dip is simple to prepare and makes a great filling for warm tortillas, pita bread, or sandwiches. Although the lemon juice helps the avocado to retain its color, the guacamole is best eaten within a few hours of making.

❶ Place the avocado in a bowl and add the lemon juice, garlic, and tomato. Mash with a fork until fairly smooth and creamy.

INGREDIENTS
1 ripe avocado, peeled, pitted, and coarsely chopped
juice of ½ lemon
1 small clove garlic, crushed
1 tomato, skinned, seeded, and diced (optional)

Pink Pasta Salad

PREPARATION TIME *5 minutes* **COOKING TIME** *10 minutes*

FREEZING *unsuitable* **MAKES** *2–4 portions*

There is now a plethora of different pasta shapes to choose from, which adds to the fun and the appeal of this quick and easy salad. Use the shrimp or salmon only if the salad can be refrigerated prior to lunchtime. If not, add diced red bell pepper and halved black grapes, which taste just as good.

❶ Cook the pasta according to the instructions on the package, until the pasta is tender, then drain well.

❷ Mix together the mayonnaise and catsup in a bowl and add the pasta, shrimp, and tomatoes. Line a container with lettuce leaves and spoon the pasta salad in the middle.

INGREDIENTS
scant 1 cup pasta shapes of your choice
2 tbsp mayonnaise
1 tbsp tomato catsup
2 oz/55 g cooked shrimp or canned pink salmon, mashed
3 cherry tomatoes, quartered
lettuce leaves, optional

Cheese Twists

PREPARATION TIME *5 minutes* **COOKING TIME** *12 minutes*

FREEZING *suitable* **MAKES** *20 twists*

These savory twists have a delicious cheesy flavor and are very tasty. They can be dipped into houmus.

❶ Preheat the oven to 400°F/200°C. Lightly grease a large cookie sheet.

❷ Mix together the Gruyère cheese and paprika and sprinkle over the sheet of puff pie dough. Fold the puff pie dough in half and roll out to seal the edges.

❸ Cut the pie dough into long ½-in/1-cm wide strips, then cut each strip in half and gently twist. Place on the prepared cookie sheet. Brush with beaten egg and bake for 10–12 minutes, or until crisp and golden. Allow to cool on a wire rack.

INGREDIENTS
butter or margarine, for greasing
¾ cup Gruyère cheese, grated
½ tsp paprika
13 oz/375 g ready-rolled puff pie dough, thawed if frozen
1 egg, beaten

Sandwiches

- Bagel with cream cheese and yeast extract
- Peanut butter with strawberry jelly
- Peanut butter with mashed banana
- Sliced cooked chicken with grated apple and mayonnaise
- Chicken and mashed banana
- Mashed tuna, avocado with mayonnaise, and a squeeze of lemon juice
- Houmus, diced tomato, and chopped, hard-cooked egg
- Sliced grilled bacon, chopped hard-cooked egg, and mayonnaise
- Ham, mashed pineapple chunks, and ricotta cheese
- Cheese scones with bacon and cream cheese
- Vegetarian sausages with tomato
- Ciabatta with a wedge of omelet
- Ciabatta with pesto, mozzarella cheese, and tomato

ABOVE *Healthy snacks and packed lunches will actually satisfy your child's appetite, and will not provide the "false energy" feeling that very sugary foods produce.*

- Sardine paté and cucumber
- Pita bread with couscous, houmus, and mint
- Pita bread pizzas

Snacks

- Raisin muffins with cream cheese
- Rice cakes with chocolate spread and sliced banana
- Nuts and raisins
- Breadsticks and dip
- Crumpets with strawberry jelly and cream cheese
- Mini pita breads spread with garlic butter and sprinkled with grated cheese and broiled
- Tortillas
- Flapjacks
- Malt loaf or fruit bread
- Fruit jello with fresh fruit
- Houmus with sticks of carrot, cucumber, and celery

Lemon Barley Water

PREPARATION TIME *5 minutes*   **COOKING TIME** *35 minutes*

FREEZING *suitable*   **MAKES** *3 pints/1.7 litres*

This homemade lemon drink is very refreshing on a hot day and is great for when your child has friends to play. It has less sugar than most store-bought versions.

❶ Rinse the barley under cold running water, then place in a large saucepan. Cover with the water and bring to a boil. Reduce the heat and simmer for 30 minutes, skimming off any froth that may appear from time to time. Remove from the heat.

INGREDIENTS
1 cup pearl barley
7½ cups water
grated rind of 1 lemon
¼ cup golden superfine sugar
juice of 2 lemons

VARIATIONS

Substitute orange rind and juice for lemon rind and juice.

❷ Add the lemon rind and sugar to the pan, stir well until the sugar has dissolved and leave to cool. Strain, then add the lemon juice. Serve chilled.

Strawberry & Banana Shake

PREPARATION TIME *5 minutes* **FREEZING** *suitable* **SERVES** *2 adults*

This creamy fruity drink can be transformed into delicious lollies
if it is frozen. You can use other fruit combinations, too.

❶ Put the bananas, strawberries,
wheatgerm, and yogurt in a
blender and process for a minute,
or until smooth and creamy. Pour
into glasses and serve.

INGREDIENTS
2 bananas, quartered
scant 2 cups strawberries, hulled and halved if large
1 tbsp wheatgerm or oatmeal
2½ cups plain live yogurt

Wiggly Noodle Soup

PREPARATION TIME *5 minutes*   **COOKING TIME** *8 minutes*
FREEZING *suitable*   **SERVES** *4 adults*

Quick, nutritious, and fun, this soup can be messy, so be
prepared! Miso is made from soy beans, which can be bought in
paste form, although here I've gone for convenience and opted for
instant miso soup that simply requires the addition of water.

❶ Bring a large pan of water to
the boil, add the noodles and
cook according to the
instructions on the package, until
the noodles are just tender. Drain
the noodles in a strainer. Rinse
under cold running water, then
drain again and set aside.

❷ Put the miso soup in a large
saucepan and bring to a boil,
then add the soy sauce.

❸ Reduce the heat and add the
snowpeas, carrot, and scallions, if
using, and simmer for 3 minutes,

INGREDIENTS
scant 2 cups egg noodles
4 cups instant miso soup
1 tbsp dark soy sauce
4 oz/115 g snow peas, thinly sliced diagonally
1 carrot, peeled and cut into fine strips
2 scallions, finely sliced (optional)
1 tbsp toasted sesame seeds (optional)
salt and freshly ground black pepper

or until the vegetables are just
tender. Season to taste.

❹ Divide the noodles between
four bowls and pour in the soup.
Sprinkle with the sesame seeds.

Honey Salmon Kebabs

PREPARATION TIME *5 minutes, plus 1 hour marinating*

COOKING TIME *5 minutes* **FREEZING** *unsuitable* **SERVES** *4 adults*

The honey-based marinade gives a wonderful, sweet, caramel flavor and glossy coating to the cubes of salmon. While kebabs are fun, do take care when giving them to children. If you use wooden skewers, soak them in water to stop them burning.

❶ Mix together the ingredients for the marinade in a shallow dish. Add the salmon and stir to coat the fish in the marinade. Let marinate in the refrigerator for 1 hour, turning the fish over in the marinade occasionally.

❷ Preheat the broiler to high. Thread the cubes of salmon on to 8 skewers. Line a broiler rack with foil and place the skewers on top. Brush the salmon with the marinade and broil for 3–5 minutes, turning the skewers occasionally, until cooked.

❸ While the salmon is cooking, put the remaining marinade in a small saucepan and heat for a few minutes until it has reduced and thickened.

❹ Serve the kebabs with rice. Spoon the reduced marinade over the salmon and sprinkle with sesame seeds, if using.

INGREDIENTS
4 boneless salmon fillets, each about 5 oz/ 140 g, skinned and cut into ¾-in/2-cm cubes
1 tbsp toasted sesame seeds (optional)

MARINADE
2 tbsp runny honey
1 tbsp soy sauce
1 tbsp olive oil
1 tsp toasted sesame oil

Sunny Rice

PREPARATION TIME *10 minutes*   **COOKING TIME** *30 minutes*

FREEZING *suitable*   **SERVES** *4 adults*

This comforting, lightly spiced rice dish is topped with slices of hard-cooked egg for extra goodness. Make sure you choose undyed smoked fish, not the artificially colored, yellow variety.

INGREDIENTS
1 lb/450 g undyed smoked haddock or cod fillets
2 cups water
generous 1 cup basmati rice, rinsed
1 bay leaf
2 cloves
4 tbsp butter
½ cup frozen baby peas
1 tsp garam masala
½ tsp ground turmeric
2 tbsp chopped flat-leaved parsley
4 hard-cooked eggs, quartered
freshly ground black pepper

❶ Put the haddock in a large skillet and pour enough milk or water over the fish to just cover it. Poach the fish for 5 minutes, or until cooked and opaque. Remove the haddock from the pan and flake the fish, carefully removing the skin and any bones. Discard the remainder of the poaching liquid.

❷ Meanwhile, place the rice in a saucepan and cover with the water, then add the bay leaf and cloves. Bring to a boil, then reduce the heat and simmer, covered, for 15 minutes, or until the water has been absorbed and the rice is tender. Discard the bay leaf and cloves. Set aside the covered pan.

❸ Melt the butter over a gentle heat in the cleaned skillet, then add the peas and cook for 2 minutes, or until tender. Stir in the garam masala and turmeric and cook for another minute.

❹ Stir in the haddock and rice and mix well until they are coated in the spiced butter.

❺ Season and heat through for 1–2 minutes. Stir in the parsley and top with the hard-cooked eggs just before serving.

Chicken, Apple & Nut Salad

PREPARATION TIME *5 minutes* **COOKING TIME** *1 minute*
FREEZING *unsuitable* **SERVES** *2 adults*

The creamy dressing and the sweetness of the apple add to the child appeal of this crunchy salad. I've included scallions, but you can easily leave them out without detriment to the flavor.

❶ Toast the pine nuts in a dry skillet until lightly golden.

❷ Toss the apple in the lemon juice to prevent the flesh from discoloring. Place the apple and any leftover lemon juice in a bowl with the chicken, celery, and scallion, if using. Add the toasted pine nuts.

❸ Mix together the mayonnaise and yogurt and spoon the dressing over the salad. Mix well to coat the salad in the dressing.

INGREDIENTS
1 tbsp pine nuts
1 red-skinned apple, cored and diced
1 tbsp lemon juice
6 oz/175 g cooked chicken breast, skinned and diced
1 celery stalk, finely chopped
1 scallion, finely chopped (optional)

DRESSING
2 tbsp mayonnaise
3 tbsp plain yogurt

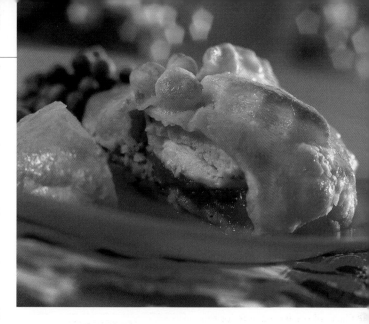

Thanksgiving Pie

PREPARATION TIME *10 minutes* **COOKING TIME** *25 minutes*
FREEZING *suitable* **MAKES** *4 adults*

These individual golden puff-pie-dough pies are full of flavors that are reminiscent of Thanksgiving.

❶ Preheat the oven to 400°F/200°C. Lay out the pie dough on a lightly floured counter. Divide the pie dough into four pieces.

❷ Season the turkey breasts and cut each one into two. Arrange the turkey fillets on top of the pie dough, leaving a border around the edge, then spoon over the chutney. Divide the stuffing in four and place it on top.

❸ Fold the long edges of the pie dough together and seal the top with water, then fold in the ends and seal. Repeat with the remaining three parcels. Cut any remaining pie dough into holly shapes and place on top of each parcel. Brush each pie with beaten egg and place on a lightly greased cookie sheet.

❹ Bake for 25 minutes, or until the pie dough is golden and the turkey is cooked inside.

INGREDIENTS
13 oz/375 g ready-rolled puff pie dough, thawed if frozen
2 skinless turkey breasts, each weighing about 4 oz/115 g
2 tbsp redcurrant chutney or cranberry jelly
5½ oz/150 g sage and onion stuffing
1 egg, beaten
salt and freshly ground black pepper

Baby Burgers

PREPARATION TIME *10 minutes* **COOKING TIME** *30 minutes*

FREEZING *suitable* **MAKES** *10 burgers*

There's something very appealing about bite-sized food and these mini burgers are no exception, fitting perfectly into those sesame or poppy seed baby rolls you can now buy. These burgers are perfect for little hands to hold and are easy to eat.

1 Place all the ingredients for the burgers, except the oil, in a large bowl and mix together with your hands until combined. Season, then shape the mixture into small balls, using your hands. Set aside in the refrigerator for 15 minutes.

2 Heat enough oil to cover the bottom of a large heavy-bottomed skillet and cook the meatballs, for 3–5 minutes, turning them occasionally, until cooked through and browned.

3 Serve the burgers in a small bun with lettuce, sliced tomato, and mayonnaise or relish.

INGREDIENTS

¾ cup fresh whole-wheat bread crumbs

1 tsp dried oregano

1 onion, grated

1 carrot, peeled and grated

1 clove garlic, crushed

3 cups lean ground beef

1 tbsp tomato paste

1 egg, beaten

vegetable oil, for frying

salt and freshly ground black pepper

TO SERVE

mini burger buns

lettuce leaves

sliced tomato

mayonnaise or relish

Chinese Omelet Roll

PREPARATION TIME *5 minutes* **COOKING TIME** *8 minutes*

FREEZING *unsuitable* **SERVES** *4 adults*

A thin, golden omelet makes a remarkably good wrapping for cooked vegetables.

❶ Blanch the broccoli in boiling water for 2 minutes, until slightly softened. Drain the broccoli, then refresh under cold running water.

❷ Heat half the oil in a wok or skillet. Add the garlic, ginger, red bell pepper, cabbage, and broccoli and stir-fry for 3 minutes, tossing the vegetables to prevent them from sticking.

❸ Add the beansprouts and cook for a further minute, then add the black bean sauce, stir and heat through. Remove from the heat and cover the wok or pan to keep the stir-fry warm.

❹ Season the beaten eggs. Heat a little of the remaining oil in a

INGREDIENTS

scant ¾ cup broccoli florets, cut into small pieces

2 tbsp groundnut oil

1 clove garlic

½-in/1-cm piece of fresh root ginger, finely grated

1 small red bell pepper, seeded and diced

scant ½ cup white cabbage, finely shredded

scant ½ cup beansprouts

2 tbsp black bean sauce

4 eggs, lightly beaten

salt and freshly ground black pepper

small skillet and add a quarter of the beaten egg. Swirl the egg to cover the base of the pan. Cook until set, then turn the omelet out on to a plate and keep warm while you make three more omelets.

❺ Spoon the vegetable stir-fry along the center of each omelet and roll it up. Cut the omelet in half crosswise.

VARIATIONS

Shrimp or chicken make a delicious addition to the cooked vegetables. If using strips of chicken, cook them in Step 2, until browned, before adding the garlic and ginger. Add the shrimp with the garlic in Step 2.

Green Giant Pasta

PREPARATION TIME *10 minutes* **COOKING TIME** *15 minutes*
FREEZING *suitable* **SERVES** *4 adults*

I've included a recipe for fresh pesto, but the store-bought variety can be used if preferred or if time is short. Pesto is a real favorite with many children and just a spoonful transforms pasta or rice.

❶ First make the pesto. Place the basil, garlic, and pine nuts in a blender and process until finely chopped. Gradually add the oil and then the Parmesan cheese and blend to a coarse purée. Season to taste. Spoon the pesto into a jar with a lid. Pour over extra olive oil to cover. Use immediately or store in the refrigerator for up to a week.

❷ Cook the pasta according to the instructions on the package, until the pasta is just tender, then drain, reserving 1–2 tablespoons of the cooking water.

❸ Meanwhile, cook the potatoes in boiling water for 10 minutes,

INGREDIENTS
generous 3 cups linguini, spaghetti, or tagliatelle
8 new potatoes, halved or quartered, if large
2 tsp olive oil
½ cup frozen baby peas
1–2 tbsp pine nuts, toasted in a dry skillet

PESTO
1 cup fresh basil leaves
2 cloves garlic, crushed
½ cup pine nuts
½ cup olive oil, plus extra for drizzling
4 tbsp freshly grated Parmesan cheese
salt and freshly ground black pepper

or until tender. Cut the potato pieces into bite-sized cubes.

❹ Heat the oil in a large saucepan, then add 4 tablespoons of pesto, the cooked potatoes, and peas. Heat the pesto mixture for a few minutes, then season to taste. Add the pasta and the reserved cooking water if it appears too dry. Heat through and mix in the pine nuts.

❺ Serve sprinkled with cheese.

Fresh Fruit Sticks

PREPARATION TIME *10 minutes* **COOKING TIME** *15 minutes*

FREEZING *unsuitable* **SERVES** *4 adults*

Children can help to assemble these colorful, vitamin-rich fruit sticks, but they do need adult supervision if they are very young. The fruit sticks can be grilled or barbecued and are excellent served with a dollop of thick plain yogurt or a good-quality vanilla ice cream. Wooden skewers are preferable, but do soak them in water for 10 minutes beforehand to prevent them burning.

❶ Preheat the broiler to high and line the broiler pan with foil. Arrange the fruit on the wooden skewers.

❷ Heat the honey or maple syrup in a small saucepan until runny and brush liberally over the kebabs using a pastry brush or your fingers, if you prefer.

❸ Broil for 5–8 minutes, or until the fruit softens and the honey or syrup begins to caramelize.

INGREDIENTS

Choose from a selection of fresh fruit: pineapples, mangoes, bananas, kiwi, peaches, and oranges are best, cut into ½-in/1-cm chunks

runny honey or maple syrup, for brushing

Little Jack Horner Pudding

PREPARATION TIME *10 minutes*   **COOKING TIME** *30 minutes*

FREEZING *unsuitable*   **SERVES** *4 adults*

This warming and comforting plum batter pudding is similar to the classic French dessert clafouti. It is best served hot with cream.

❶ Preheat the oven to 400°F/200°C.

❷ Beat the eggs, egg yolk, and sugar in a large bowl until light and frothy. Stir in the vanilla extract and flour with a wooden spoon and beat until smooth.

❸ Mix together the melted butter, sour cream, and milk and add to the bowl. Gently stir until combined.

❹ Arrange the plums in the bottom of a lightly buttered 8 in/20 cm ovenproof dish, then pour the egg mixture over the fruit. Bake for 25–30 minutes, or until risen and set.

INGREDIENTS
2 eggs
1 egg yolk
scant ½ cup superfine sugar
1 tsp vanilla extract
½ cup all-purpose flour, sifted
3 tbsp sweet butter, melted, plus extra for greasing
⅓ cup sour cream
¼ cup whole milk
3 plums, pitted and coarsely chopped

Gingerbread People

PREPARATION TIME *10 minutes*

COOKING TIME *12 minutes*

FREEZING *unsuitable*

MAKES *6 people, or more depending on the size of cutter*

INGREDIENTS
1½ cups all-purpose flour
2 tsp ground ginger
½ tsp bicarbonate of soda
4 tbsp butter or margarine
6 tbsp brown sugar
2 tbsp corn syrup
1 egg, beaten
TO DECORATE
Royal icing, piping consistency
Chocolate beans or raisins

Children love helping to make these golden gingerbread men and women.

❶ Preheat the oven to 375°F/190°C. Sift the flour, ginger, and bicarbonate of soda into a large mixing bowl. Add the butter and rub into the flour with your fingers until the mixture resembles fine bread crumbs. Mix in the sugar.

❷ Warm the syrup in a small saucepan until runny, then add to the flour mixture with the beaten egg. Mix to form a soft dough, then knead lightly until smooth. If the dough is too sticky, add a little extra flour.

❸ Roll out the dough on a lightly floured counter then, using a cutter, make the gingerbread people. Place on a lightly greased cookie sheet and cook for 10 minutes, or until just crisp and golden. Allow to cool.

❹ Pipe small blobs of icing to make a face and buttons on each person. Use the chocolate beans or raisins for eyes and buttons.

Passion Cake Squares

PREPARATION TIME *15 minutes*   **COOKING TIME** *1 hour*

FREEZING *unsuitable*   **MAKES** *1 cake*

This moist, light carrot cake couldn't be easier to make and is a delicious way to encourage your child to eat vegetables!

❶ Preheat the oven to 350°F/180°C. Lightly grease a 8-in/20-cm square cake pan and line the base with waxed paper.

❷ Sift the flour and salt into a large mixing bowl. Add the spices, sugar, carrots, and dates and mix well until combined.

❸ Stir together the beaten eggs and oil, then pour into the mixing bowl and beat until thoroughly combined.

❹ Pour the slightly lumpy mixture into the prepared tin and bake for 1 hour, or until a toothpick inserted into the center of the cake comes out clean. Leave for 5 minutes, then carefully turn out the cake and allow to cool completely on a wire rack.

❺ To make the frosting, beat the cream cheese, butter, and vanilla

INGREDIENTS
2 cups self-rising flour
pinch of salt
1 tsp ground cinnamon
1 tsp ground nutmeg
1 cup brown sugar
1½ cups carrots, peeled and finely grated
generous ½ cup dried, ready-to-eat dates, coarsely chopped
3 eggs, lightly beaten
¾ cup sunflower oil

FROSTING
½ cup cream cheese
4 tbsp butter
1 tsp vanilla extract
scant 2 cups confectioner's sugar

extract together until smooth and creamy. Beat in the sugar and store the frosting in the fridge for 20 minutes to harden slightly. Spread the frosting over the cake and cut it into small squares.

VARIATIONS
Substitute finely grated zucchini for the carrot and add 1 tbsp pine nuts or chopped walnuts.

Useful Websites and Organizations

These provide information on childcare and nutrition, and can help you if you have any questions or concerns.

USEFUL WEBSITES

kidshealth.org

A useful site with sections on feeding your toddler: feeding your 1–2 year old, deciphering food labels, healthy mealtime habits, nutrients your child needs and packing school lunches.

www.allhealth.com

This site gives information on school-age nutrition, an area that often worries parents because their children come under different influences when they start full-time education.

www.abcparenting.com

General information on feeding toddlers and coping with their first time at school.

babyparenting.about.com

Information on child nutrition and health.

www.babycenter.com

Information on toddler behavior and development, toddler health, feeding, nutrition and breastfeeding your toddler.

www.kidsource.com

Addresses health and diseases issues, and the correct kind of preventive care. Also deals with nutritional questions.

www.drgreene.com/ toddlers.html

Information on the effect of sugar on behaviour and the value of vegetables—plus advice on handling temper tantrums.

www.uri.edu/coopext/efnep/ toddlers/toddler.p4.html

Information on the characteristics of the toddler, feeding the toddler, appropriate foods and amounts for toddlers and a guide to the appropriate serving sizes.

www.findarticles.com

A collection of recipes for nutritious and tasty children's breakfasts to replace sugar-coated cereal and milk.

www.pampers.com

Offers tips for enticing toddlers at every developmental stage to participate in meals.

www.parentsoup.com
Find answers to common questions about toddler nutrition. Includes advice for parents of picky eaters and tips on weaning.

www.parentsplace.com
Expert advice on issues such as lactose intolerance, pickiness and food allergies. Also contains toddler nutrition guidelines, information on picky eaters, feeding guidelines, nutritional guidelines, vegetarian issues, allergies and sensitivities and food safety.

www.diapernet.com/diqa/ diqas19.htm
Encouraging toddlers to eat a variety of foods: suggestions from parents on getting toddlers to stray from their favorite foods.

www.thecybermom.com
Features resources on tons of toddler-related subjects, including useful information on food preferences and picky eating.

www.mothersnature.com
Post a question about toddler behavior or development or scan the boards for advice on a range of topics.

www.toddlerstoday.com
News related to toddlers, along with articles, an expert Q&A and parent diaries.

USEFUL ORGANIZATIONS

Association of Breastfeeding Mothers
abm@clara.net
http://home.clara.net/abm/
Offers breastfeeding advice and information, and trains breastfeeding counselors.

Beyond the Baby Blues
www.babyblues.freeserve.co.uk
Offers an easily accessible, confidential support network for mothers who are suffering from postnatal depression.

Centre for Pregnancy Nutrition
pregnancy.nutrition@sheffield. ac.uk
Helpline: (+44) 0114 2424084

Fathers Direct
www.fathersdirect.com
mail@fathersdirect.com
Promotes close and positive relationships between men and their children from infancy. Aims to break down barriers that exist in society that make it difficult for fathers to develop such relationships with their children.

Parentline Plus
www.parentline.co.uk
Helpline: (+44) 0808 800 2222
Offers support to anyone who is parenting a child—the child's parents, step-parents, grandparents, and foster parents. Provides a range of information.

Index

Acknowledgements

The author would like to thank the following:

The Institute of Child Health, London; The Health Education Authority, London; The Department of Health, London.

The publishers would like to thank the following for permission to reproduce copyright material: Bubbles: pp. 6, 36, 39, 69; Getty Stone: pp. 4, 7, 8; Image Bank: pp. 9, 10, 13, 24, 37, 66; Superstock: pp. 5, 14.